# Level 1
# Workbook 2

**This workbook accompanies Slipstream Level 1 books**

Rollercoaster $31,000,000

EDGE
W FRANKLIN WATTS
**LONDON·SYDNEY**

## Roger Hurn

First published in 2013 by
Franklin Watts
338 Euston Road
London NW1 3BH

Franklin Watts Australia
Level 17/207 Kent Street
Sydney NSW 2000

© Franklin Watts 2013

ISBN 978 1 4451 1798 0

A CIP catalogue record for this book
is available from the British Library.

Series Editors: Adrian Cole and Jackie Hamley
Series Advisors: Diana Bentley and Dee Reid
Series Designer: Peter Scoulding
Editorial Assistant: Amanda Marzolf

Printed in UK by Hobbs the Printers Ltd

Franklin Watts is a division of
Hachette Children's Books,
an Hachette UK company.
www.hachette.co.uk

Acknowledgements:
Blue Orange Studio/Shutterstock: 25.
Elenarts/Shutterstock: 29.
Greg Amptman/Shutterstock: 24r.
GSFC STSCI/NASA: 44t.
Gustavo Fernandes/Dreamstime: 24m.
JPL/NASA: 44mb.
Marcel Clemens/Shutterstock: 44mt, 44b.
Morrison/Shutterstock: 28.
Natursports/Shutterstock: 14b.
Paul Topp/Dreamstime: 24l.

Every attempt has been made to
clear copyright. Should there be any
inadvertent omission, please apply
to the publisher for rectification.

# Contents

# TITLES AT THIS LEVEL

## Fiction

978 1 4451 1815 4 pb

978 1 4451 1814 7 pb

978 1 4451 1816 1 pb

## Graphic fiction

978 1 4451 1803 1 pb

978 1 4451 1802 4 pb

978 1 4451 1804 8 pb

## Non-fiction

978 1 4451 1957 1

978 1 4451 1955 7

978 1 4451 1956 4

# Introduction

The worksheets included in this workbook are designed to be used as comprehension exercises in conjunction with the Slipstream Level 1 books. Some worksheets also provide the opportunity for structured but creative responses to the stories and information.

The Slipstream books are designed for students with lower level reading skills. Such students may have experiential, oral and imaginative abilities that go beyond their skills in reading and writing. This can lead to frustration, which can be exacerbated if the interest level of a text, or a worksheet level, is pitched too low. These worksheets are designed to appeal to such students by providing a range of activities that go beyond straightforward comprehension.

Each sheet is supported by teacher's notes, which provide details of the task and appropriate ways to introduce it to students. Extension ideas are provided for students who are able to use the ideas on the sheet as the basis for a more extended activity.

We recommend that the sheets are worked through as a class or group to ensure the students fully understand the instructions and have the opportunity to ask questions. For weaker students this process might involve working through the sheet individually before providing additional support, such as a vocabulary list.

# Teacher's Notes

## General worksheets

### Worksheet 1: What I Liked Best

**Task:**
To write a review of their favourite Slipstream book suggesting ways in which the book could be made even more enjoyable. Students are also asked to think of a book that they would like to write.

**Support:**
Read through the worksheet together. Discuss why they liked the book and why that particular genre appeals to them. Ask them to expand on what their own "Slipstream" title would be about.

**Extension:**
Students could discuss why they chose a particular book as their favourite. They could debate the merits of both fiction and non-fiction books and why both serve different but equally important purposes.

### Worksheet 2: Fact and Fiction

**Task:**
To understand the key differences between fiction and non-fiction books.

**Support:**
Discuss why fiction books use illustrations while many non-fiction books use photographs. Make sure the students have grasped the key differences between fiction and non-fiction books. Discuss why both types of book are of equal merit.

**Extension activity:**
Write a proposal for either a fiction book or a non-fiction book. This can be done either individually or as paired or group work.

## Wolfhold

### Worksheet 3: What Do You Remember?

**Task:**
To retell the story of *Wolfhold* in note form.

**Support:**
Recap the whole story orally.

If necessary create a word bank on the white board to support the pupil's writing.

Chapter 1 is already completed, so model writing notes for the second chapter as a whole class activity. Now have the pupils complete the notes for each chapter.

**Extension:**
Ask the pupils to complete similar notes for one of the other Slipstream fiction titles.

## Wolfhold

### Worksheet 4: What Are Tom and Megan Thinking?

**Task:**
To discuss what the characters Tom and Megan are thinking and to write their thoughts in the form of thought bubbles.

**Support:**
Discuss what Tom and Megan might be thinking about at this stage in the story. For example, think about how the shock of seeing Megan change into a werewolf would affect Tom. Why would Megan be pleased that Tom is now a werewolf? List any key vocabulary.

**Extension activity:**
Extend the thought bubble ideas into a blog entry where Tom writes down his feelings about what has happened to him.

## White Water Wipe Out!

### Worksheet 1: TV News Report

**Task:**
To complete a storyboard for a TV news report.

**Support:**
Discuss how a TV report is structured and what might be included and why. Use the storyboard to make notes of the key points. These can then be expanded into a full script on separate sheets.

**Extension activity:**
Pupils can act out the TV report as part of a group work. They can also do a follow up report on what happened next. For example, did Rick get into serious trouble for disobeying Mr Brown? Did Ali receive an award for rescuing Rick? What did Rick learn from going to the Hell Hole by himself? How upset were Rick's parents; how proud were Ali's parents?

## White Water Wipe Out!

### Worksheet 2: Beware of the Hell Hole!

**Task:**
To identify three reasons why the Hell Hole is too dangerous a stretch of water for beginners.

**Support:**
Look at the illustration on page 17 and encourage the pupils to describe what they see. What elements of the Hell Hole make it particularly dangerous?

**Extension:**
The pupils could draw up a list of rules that everyone who goes kayaking on white water must obey in order to stay safe.

## Robbed!

### Worksheet 1: Lizzie's Big Mistake

**Task:**
Retelling why Lizzie thought Big Alex was a thief.

**Support:**
Talk through the reasons why Lizzie came to the conclusion that Big Alex had robbed her brother. Discuss how the author set up events to make it look like Big Alex was guilty. Why would Tommy be cross with her?

**Extension activity:**
The completed dialogue can be performed as a play. The pupils can also discuss why it is important to be in possession of all the facts before making a judgement about a person or an event.

## Robbed!

### Worksheet 2: To Catch a Thief

**Task:**
Retelling the story in the pupils' own words using picture clues.

**Support:**
This is a straightforward activity but make sure the pupils have understood the main points of the narrative before starting and, if necessary, write up a list of useful vocabulary.

**Extension:**
Work on a retelling exercise from the point of view of Big Alex.

## Daring Escapes

### Worksheet 1: They Did What?!

**Task:**
Identifying what some of the people in the book had to do to survive.

**Support:**
This is a straightforward task. Check that the pupils have read the book carefully before asking them to complete both parts of the worksheet.

**Extension:**
Pupils can research some more incredible examples of people surviving against the odds. For example, in 1982, Steven Callahan set sail from the Canary Islands on a small boat he built himself. The boat sank six days into the trip, and Steven was left adrift on a tiny life raft. With only 1.3 kilograms of food and three litres of water, a solar still and a makeshift spear, Steven managed to survive until his rescue 76 days later.

This can developed into a group activity whereby pupils present their examples of daring escapes to the rest of the group. When each pupil has made their presentation, the group can vote to decide which of the escapes is the most amazing!

## Daring Escapes

### Worksheet 2: To Surf or Not to Surf

**Task:**
To have the pupils give an opinion on a subject and to write a sentence explaining why they feel this way.

**Support:**
Discuss with the pupils the reasons why someone may want to carry on doing a sport even though they have suffered a serious injury from participating in it. Have them consider carefully the arguments for and against such a course of action.

**Extension:**
The pupils could choose a subject about which they feel strongly and then write a short persuasive piece arguing their case.

## How to Spend a Billion

### Worksheet 1: Money Can Buy You These!

**Task:**
Identifying the item from the clues provided.

Deciding which of the items in the book they would buy if they could only chose one. Giving reasons for their choice. Making a Top Five list of the things they would buy if they had a billion dollars to spend.

**Support:**
The pupils may be unfamiliar with these huge numbers so make sure they understand the amounts they are dealing with. For example, one million has 6 zeros and one billion has 9.

Discuss how hard it is to spend a billion dollars. Talk about the type of things they would chose to buy and why they want these things.

**Extension:**
Ask the pupils to share their lists with the rest of the class and then have a vote to decide which item is the most sought after/useful/beneficial.

## How to Spend a Billion

### Worksheet 2: Making a Difference

**Task:**
Selecting three good causes to support and why. Deciding how much money to give each one.

**Support:**
Discuss with the pupils the saying that money can't buy you happiness. Then talk about the wide range of deserving causes they could choose to donate money to. Ask them to select the three that they wish to support. Encourage them to give their reasons why they have selected these causes.

**Extension:**
The pupils could make a presentation to the rest of the class explaining why their chosen charity is worthy of support.

Pupils could debate the most effective and practical ways in which they could raise money for their charities. Then they could organise and hold a fund-raising event to support the charities they have chosen.

## Space

### Worksheet 1: The Space Quiz

**Task:**
This is a straightforward task which requires the pupils to read the book *Space* and answer simple questions using the information found there.

**Support:**
Review the worksheet with the pupils and ensure that they understand the questions. This task could initially be undertaken as an oral group activity.

**Extension:**
Pupils could create a quiz of their own based on another non-fiction book in the Slipstream series. They could make this quiz a multiple choice quiz.

## Space

### Worksheet 2: Amazing News From Space!

**Task:**
Part 1 – To write a factual front page newspaper story about space exploration.

Part 2 – To write a fictional newspaper report about an alien space craft landing on Earth.

**Support:**
Look at the format of a newspaper's front page. Discuss how the headline should be attention grabbing and written in capital letters.

Explain to the pupils that the 5 Ws (What; When; Where; Who; Why) are the secret of writing an

interesting newspaper report. Point out that their report should answer these questions:

What happened?
When did it happen?
Where did it happen?
Who was involved?
Why did it happen?

Encourage the pupils to use books or the Internet to find out about the subject of space exploration. For example, the NASA kid's club is a useful source of information as is the BBC's space website.

*   http://www.nasa.gov/audience/ forkids/kidsclub/flash/index.html

*   http://www.bbc.co.uk/science/space

**Extension:**
Pupils could research and write a newspaper report about a subject of their own choice. You could turn your classroom into a newspaper office and assign roles such as editor, sub editor, reporter, photographer, features editor, etc to the pupils. You could then work together to produce a class newspaper. To prepare the children for this you and they could:

*   look at examples of different newspapers both local and national to decide what kind of newspaper your class wants to produce

*   look at what type of things make up the content of a newspaper

*   examine what each newspaper considers to be newsworthy

*   look at the way newspapers grab the reader's attention and present information to them

*   examine how newspapers make use of graphics

- explore how each newspaper tries to present its own particular view of the world

- investigate who the potential readership is for their class newspaper and what content might appeal to that readership

- discuss and agree with the pupils the type of stories and events their paper will cover

- invite the editor or a journalist from the local paper along to the school to talk to the pupils about what they do and how they do it

- arrange for the class to visit a local newspaper's offices to see it in action

## Assassin City

### Worksheet 1: True or False

**Task:**
To demonstrate understanding of the story by identifying true or false statements correctly.

**Support:**
Ensure the pupils have grasped the essential plot of the story. The false statements are 2,4,6,9 and 10.

The true and false sentences could be used as an oral group exercise in which other pupils have to work out whether they are true or not.

**Extension:**
Both Kira and Milo hate being assassins but they "assassinate" the Council. Encourage the pupils to debate the morality of their actions. Does the end justify the means in this case? Can the end ever justify the means?

## Assassin City

### Worksheet 2: Character Card

**Task:**
To design a character card for Kira.

**Support:**
Make sure the pupils have a clear understanding of the kind of character Kira is. She is an excellent assassin but she is also very troubled by what she is being forced to do. Discuss why that is and why it is only when Milo arrives that she turns against the Council.

**Extension:**
Pupils can design character cards for the other characters in the story, e.g. Raff, the combat trainer.

## Sword of Legend

### Worksheet 1: Finding the Sword

**Task:**
To show understanding of the events of the story by writing the thoughts of the characters.

**Support:**
Explain the convention of speech and thought bubbles.

The thought bubbles for Prince Hans and his father are the most challenging. Pupils may benefit from discussing the reasons why Hans lies to his father and why his father doesn't tell Hans how to summon the Sword Spirit.

**Extension:**
Encourage the pupils to read the book again and to identify places where thought bubbles could be used to give a greater insight into what the characters are feeling.

## Sword of Legend

## Worksheet 2: Wishing on a Sword

**Task:**
To think of a wish for the Sword Spirit to grant.

To supply a reason for asking for this wish.

**Support:**
Prince Hans asks the Sword Spirit to help make his father better. This is an unselfish wish. Discuss why the Sword Spirit is only likely to grant unselfish wishes. What evidence is there in the text that the Sword Spirit only responds to people with good intentions? Ask the pupils if they think the Sword Spirit would have helped Sir Murdlan if he had found the Sword of Legend before Prince Hans. Have them give reasons for their answer.

**Extension:**
Ask the pupils to think of three unselfish wishes that they would ask a magical creature like the Sword Spirit to grant.

## Switch Face

## Worksheet 1: Two Faced

**Task:**
To show understanding of the story by identifying the key incidents.

**Support:**
Work through the story with the pupils to ensure that they have grasped the major events and ideas. For example:

- Luke can change his face

- He uses this power to humiliate others

- This ability backfires

- He is unable to change his face back because of the handcuffs

**Extension:**
Ask the pupils who they would like to look like and why?

## Switch Face

## Worksheet 2: What Happened Next?

**Task:**
To write an imaginative extension of the story.

**Support:**
Discuss Luke's dilemma with the pupils. If he doesn't rub his face he will be sent to prison for crimes he didn't commit and a dangerous criminal will remain at large. However, if he does rub his face he will have to admit to all the bad things he has done.

Encourage them to think up a plausible explanation that Luke can use to explain why he is in the cell and not Finn Sampson. For example, an accomplice of Sampson's grabbed Luke, then sneaked him into the police station and forced him to take Sampson's place.

**Extension:**
Have the pupils describe how the police react to Luke's explanation. They can do this pictorially using both thought and speech bubbles. This activity can be done either individually or as part of group work.

**Name:** _____  **Date:** _____

## WHAT I LIKED BEST

I am going to write about the Slipstream book I liked best.

It's called: _____

The author is: _____

It is a fiction / non-fiction / graphic fiction book (Circle one answer.)

I really liked this book because: _____

_____

_____

The author could make this book even more fun to read if they:

_____

_____

If I were an author I would write a Slipstream book called:

_____

The book would be a fiction / non-fiction / graphic fiction book

(Circle one answer.)

Here is a sentence I've written that tells you about my book.

_____

_____

**Name:** _____ **Date:** _____

## FACT AND FICTION

We use non-fiction books to find out facts about things.
Facts are details about something that is real.

Choose three different Slipstream non-fiction books
and write down a fact from each one.

A fact about _____

A fact about _____

A fact about _____

We choose fiction books when we want to read a story that
an author has made up from their imagination.

*Wolfhold* is a fiction book.
Write a sentence that explains how you know it is a made up story.

I know *Wolfhold* is a made up story because: _____

_____

Write a sentence about a story you would like to make up from your
imagination:

_____

_____

Name: _____    Date: _____

## FACT AND FICTION

**Many fiction books and non-fiction books have pictures.**

**The Slipstream fiction books have illustrations drawn by an illustrator.
The Slipstream non-fiction books have photographs taken by a camera.**

**Write two sentences to say why you think this is.**

Fiction books have illustrations because _____

_____

_____

_____

Many non-fiction books have photographs because _____

_____

_____

_____

_____

**Name:** _____ **Date:** _____

## WHAT DO YOU REMEMBER?

Look at the illustrations below. Then fill in the blanks based on what you remember from reading the book.

### Chapter 1

When Tom wakes up he is in a strange place. He meets a girl called Megan. He thinks he was in a fight but he can't remember.

### Chapter 2

Tom can't buy a _____ or use the _____. Tom wants to go _____. Megan says there is no way out of _____.

### Chapter 3

Tom sets off across the _____. He comes to a high _____. Megan tells him to come back to the _____.

### Chapter 4

The moon was _____. The villagers came to the huge _____. They change into _____. Wolfhold is a _____. Tom is a _____ too.

# 04 Fiction – Wolfhold
## Worksheet 2 – What Are Tom And Megan Thinking?

Name: _____ Date: _____

# WHAT ARE TOM AND MEGAN THINKING?

Tom is in a very scary situation!
What are he and Megan thinking?

**Name:** _____ **Date:** _____

## TV NEWS REPORT

Ali's dramatic rescue of Rick from the Hell Hole has made the TV news.
Use this storyboard to plan the script of the TV news report.

**Introduction by the TV reporter**

Early this morning, a young man called Rick had his life saved by his friend, Ali. Rick was kayaking on a wild stretch of river known as the Hell Hole. Here's what happened.

**Rick said**

_____

_____

_____

_____

**Mr Brown, the boys' instructor, said**

_____

_____

_____

_____

_____

_____

_____

_____

**Summary by the TV reporter**

# 06 Fiction – White Water Wipe Out!
## Worksheet 2 – Beware of the Hell Hole!

**SLIP STREAM**

Name: _____  Date: _____

## BEWARE OF THE HELL HOLE!

Do you remember that Mr Brown said the
Hell Hole was too dangerous for beginners?

Look carefully at the picture on page 17. Now write down three reasons
why beginners should never go near the Hell Hole.

**1** _____

**2** _____

**3** _____

**Name:** _____  **Date:** _____

## LIZZIE'S BIG MISTAKE

After Lizzie accused Big Alex of robbing her brother, she had to confess and admit her mistake.

**Fill in the imagined dialogue between Lizzie and Tommy.**

> I made a bad mistake today. My brother Tommy had been robbed and I accused Big Alex of being the thief – but he wasn't!

**TOMMY:** Why did you say Big Alex was a thief?

**LIZZIE:** Because I knew you'd been robbed.

**TOMMY:** I had, but that doesn't mean Big Alex did it!

**LIZZIE:** No, but... _____

_____

**TOMMY:** _____

_____

**LIZZIE:** Yes, but when I saw him... _____

_____

_____

**TOMMY:** _____

_____

_____

**LIZZIE:** _____

_____

_____

**TOMMY:** _____

_____

Name: _____ Date: _____

## TO CATCH A THIEF - PART 1

This story starts out with Lizzie thinking Big Alex has robbed her brother but she couldn't be more wrong!

**Use the picture clues to tell your version of the story.**

Tommy was late. Lizzie ... _____

_____

Then Lizzie saw ... _____

_____

Tommy's cash card was not ... _____

_____

A boy on a bike told Lizzie that ... _____

_____

Big Alex was taking Tommy to ... _____

_____

Lizzie yelled ... _____

_____

She pushed Big Alex ... _____

_____

Tommy told Lizzie that ... _____

_____

Name: _____ Date: _____

## TO CATCH A THIEF – PART 2

Big Alex had … _____

_____

Big Alex said a girl was offering a reward of fifty

pounds for a … _____

_____

The boy held out the … _____

_____

Big Alex took … _____

_____

Tommy put out his leg and … _____

_____

Alex held his hand out for the … _____

_____

Big Alex told Lizzie to … _____

_____

**SLIP STREAM**

Name: _____ Date: _____

## THEY DID WHAT?! – PART 1
Read *Daring Escapes* carefully and see if you can find out what the people in the book did to survive.

When a plane crashed in Chile the survivors had to …

_____

_____

Ricky Megee survived in the Australian outback by …

_____

_____

Aron Ralston escaped from under a rock by …

_____

_____

When a shark bit off Bethany Hamilton's arm she …

_____

_____

**SLIP STREAM**

Name: _____    Date: _____

# THEY DID WHAT?! – PART 2
Two of the daring escapes in the book have been missed out from part 1.
Find out which ones they are.

**Now choose the one you think is the most daring and write three of your own sentences describing what happened to the people involved.**

1 _____

_____

2 _____

_____

3 _____

_____

**Name:** _____  **Date:** _____

## TO SURF OR NOT TO SURF
A shark bit off Bethany Hamilton's arm when she was surfing.
Bethany loves to surf so she still goes surfing!

### Do you think this is a good idea?

I think it is a good / bad idea.  (Circle one answer.)

### Write a sentence to say why you would, or would not, go surfing again if a shark had bitten off your arm.

I _____ go surfing again because _____

_____

_____

Name: _____  Date: _____

# MONEY CAN BUY YOU THESE! – PART 1
### Read *How to Spend a Billion* and then answer the questions below.

Which arch enemy of Doctor Who can you buy for $5,000?

_____

What tasty fast-food meal can you buy with $6,000?

I can buy _____

Which footballer will play for your team for $140,000,000?

_____

How much will it cost to buy your own island?

It will cost _____

Which mode of transport will cost you $200,000 and doesn't even have an engine?

_____

How much will you have to pay for a seat on the first tourist trip to the Moon?

_____

Which cuddly creatures can be your pets for $1,488,000?

_____

**SLIP STREAM**

Name: _____  Date: _____

# MONEY CAN BUY YOU THESE! – PART 2

Which of the things in the book would you buy if you could choose just one?

I would buy _____

Why would you buy this?

I would buy this because _____

_____

_____

Make a list of the top five things you would buy if you had one billion dollars to spend.

### My Billion Dollar Top Five List of Things to Buy

1. _____

2. _____

3. _____

4. _____

5. _____

Name: _____ Date: _____

## MAKING A DIFFERENCE

Even after buying all the things in the book you still have
$62,781,000 left to spend!

There are lots of good causes that need money. Choose three
good causes you would give money to. Why have you chosen
these good causes? How much will you give to each one?

**My first good cause is** _____

I have chosen this cause because _____

_____

I will give them _____


**My second good cause is** _____

I have chosen this cause because _____

_____

I will give them _____


**My third good cause is** _____

I have chosen this cause because _____

_____

I will give them _____

**Name:** _____ **Date:** _____

# THE SPACE QUIZ – PART 1

There are no prizes for this quiz about space but if you
get all the answers right you'll be a super star!

**1** How many planets are there in the solar system?

There are _____

**2** What is the Sun?

The Sun is a _____

**3** When did the first people land on the Moon?

The first people landed on the Moon in _____

**4** What killed off the dinosaurs?

A huge _____

**5** What have we sent to explore Mars?

We have sent _____

**6** What are the outer planets made of?

They are made of _____

Name: _____ Date: _____

# THE SPACE QUIZ - PART 2

**1** What is Voyager carrying?

It is carrying _____

**2** What is our galaxy called?

It is called _____

**3** How many stars are there in the Milky Way?

There are _____

**4** What may some exoplanets have on them?

They probably have _____

**5** What might aliens spot?

They may spot _____

**6** Why do people float around in space?

They float around because _____

Name: _____ Date: _____

## AMAZING NEWS FROM SPACE! – PART 1

Imagine that you just discovered a new planet in space.
Write up the news report below, and draw an image of the planet.

**The Planet**

**Amazing News From Space!**

EDGE
LONDON•SYDNEY

Name: _____ Date: _____

## AMAZING NEWS FROM SPACE! – PART 2
Imagine an alien spacecraft has just landed in your town!
Write a newspaper report about what happened next.

# Aliens have landed!
## A report by our ace reporter on the scene.

First _____

_____

Next _____

_____

Then _____

_____

After that _____

_____

When _____

_____

In the end _____

_____

**Name:** _____  **Date:** _____

# TRUE OR FALSE – PART 1

These sentences are about the story *Assassin City*.

Are they true or false?
Circle the correct answer.

1. The Council gave Milo a job as an assassin. **True / False**

2. Milo was happy to be an assassin. **True / False**

3. The combat trainer had a big moustache. **True / False**

4. Milo's first job was to kill a terrorist. **True / False**

5. The Council were protected by a fire-resistant shield. **True / False**

6. Kira refused to help Milo. **True / False**

7. Kira pretended to need a hand with her body armour. **True / False**

**Name:** _____  **Date:** _____

## TRUE OR FALSE – PART 2

8.     Milo changed the fire power to freeze power.

**True / False**

9.     The Council watched Milo from behind

a fence.  **True / False**

10.    Kira said it was time for tea in Alpha City.

**True / False**

**Write your own true and false sentences.**

A *true* sentence about *Assassin City* :

_____

_____

A *false* sentence about *Assassin City* :

_____

_____

**Name:** _____ **Date:** _____

## CHARACTER CARD
### Make a character card for Kira the Assassin.

Assassin's name:

Where she lives:

Trained by:

Appearance:

Skills:

Favourite weapon:

Likes:

Dislikes:

Assassin rating:

**Name:** _____ **Date:** _____

## FINDING THE SWORD – PART 1
### What are Prince Hans and Sir Murdlan thinking?
**Write their thoughts in the bubbles.**

LONDON•SYDNEY

Name: _____ Date: _____

## FINDING THE SWORD – PART 2

**What are Prince Hans and his father thinking?**

**What are Prince Hans and Sir Murdlan thinking?**

Name: _____ Date: _____

## WISHING ON A SWORD
Hans asks the Sword Spirit to help his father.

**What would you ask the Sword Spirit to do
if you owned the Sword of Legend?**

**Why would you ask this?**

I would ask the Sword Spirit _____

_____

_____

I would ask this because _____

_____

_____

_____

_____

**SLIP STREAM**

Name: _____ Date: _____

## TWO FACED

Luke uses his amazing power to make trouble for others.
**Write the bad things he did. The first one is done for you.**

**First Luke threw eggs at a teacher.**

Then he changed his face to look like the Headteacher and made all the pupils

_____

Next he pretended to be _____

After that he _____

Finally it all went wrong for Luke when he changed into _____

_____

**Why couldn't Luke rub his face and turn back into himself?**

Luke couldn't rub his face because _____

_____

_____

# 20 Graphic Fiction – Switch Face
## Worksheet 2 – What Happened Next?

**Name:** _____   **Date:** _____

## WHAT HAPPENED NEXT?

When the police remove the handcuffs, Luke will be able to
rub his face and change back into himself.

**What story will he tell to explain why he is in the cell and not Finn Sampson?**

# Games and Activities

## Worksheet 1: The Hell Hole

**Task:**
To play a simple board game.

**Support:**
Explain the rules of the game.

- Roll a dice to start

- Do what it says if they land on a bonus or forfeit square

- Players must throw the exact number to reach the finish

**Extension:**
Pupils can make their own board game based on one of the other Slipstream titles.

## Worksheet 2: Joined Up Sentences

**Task:**
To correctly match up the two halves of each sentence.

**Support:**
Have the pupils reread the book *Robbed!* so that they can see the action the first half of each sentence is describing.

**Extension:**
Ask the pupils to choose another Slipstream fiction or graphic fiction book and write four sentences from it that describe four incidents from the story. Then have them cut the sentences in half, jumble them up and give them to a partner to join together correctly.

## Worksheet 3: Planet Match Up

**Task:**
To match the planet names to the correct planet.

**Support:**
Read through *Space* and make sure the pupils are aware of the different planets and what they look like.

**Extension:**
Pupils can make their own match-up activity using pictures from magazines.

## Worksheet 4: Planet Scramble

**Task:**
To rearrange the letters to form the names of the eight planets in our solar system.

**Support:**
Point out that each of the scrambled words has a capital letter in it. This is the letter

# Games and Activities

they need to put at the start of the word in order to help identify the planet.

**Extension:**
Pupils can scramble the names of their favourite football teams, celebrities or TV programmes, and see if other pupils can unscramble them and correctly identify them.

## Worksheet 5: Million Dollar Wordsearch

**Task:**
To find the four items that cost a million dollars or more in the wordsearch.

**Support:**
Words appear horizontally, vertically and diagonally.

The four items are:

- Pandas
- Island
- Ship
- Spacesuit

**Extension:**
Make up their own wordsearch.

## Worksheet 6: Two of a Kind

**Task:**
To match up identical pictures.

**Support:**
Some pupils may find it helpful to see the images in position before they are turned over at the start of the game.

**Extension:**
Have them think up another memory game. What strategies can they make use of to aid their memory?

## Worksheet 5: Write Your Own Script

**Task:**
To write a new graphic fiction story using this page and the speech bubbles as a starting point.

**Support:**
Discuss the limitations of the bubbles (size, who is speaking, reading order) and what that means for their script.

**Extension:**
Look at examples of other graphic novels. What conventions make up a graphic novel, and how can they use them when creating their own stories?

**Name:** _____     **Date:** _____

# THE HELL HOLE

Roll a dice to launch your kayak. Select a play piece and move it along the board, following the numbers. Do what each square instructs you to do. The first player to square 25 is the winner!

## THE HELL HOLE

| | | | | |
|---|---|---|---|---|
| **1**<br><br>**Start** | **2** | **3**<br><br>You lose a paddle. Miss a turn. | **4** | **5**<br><br>You have forgotten your lifejacket! Go back to the start. |
| **10**<br><br>You're caught in a whirlpool! Miss two turns! | **9** | **8** | **7**<br><br>White water! Move foward four squares. | **6** |
| **11** | **12** | **13**<br><br>Your kayak overturns. Miss one turn. | **14** | **15** |
| **20** | **19**<br><br>You hit a rock. Go back two squares. | **18** | **17** | **16**<br><br>You paddle hard. Have another throw. |
| **21**<br><br>Fast current. Move on two squares. | **22** | **23** | **24**<br><br>You are in the Hell Hole. It's a white water wipe out! Go back to start! | **25**<br><br>**Finish**<br><br>Well done! You've beaten the Hell Hole. |

**02** Fiction – Robbed!
Games and Activities – Joined Up Sentences

Name: _____ Date: _____

## JOINED UP SENTENCES

Cut out these boxes and then join the sentences together so they match.

| | |
|---|---|
| Lizzie pushes Big Alex | if they've seen Tommy. |
| Alex takes a photo | not to call him Big Alex. |
| Lizzie asks lots of kids | and tripped him up. |
| Alex tells Lizzie | away from her brother. |
| Tommy put his leg out | of the thief. |

Name: _____     Date: _____

## PLANET MATCH UP
Cut out and then match the planet picture to the correct name.

| Jupiter |
| --- |

| Mars |
| --- |

| Earth |
| --- |

| Saturn |
| --- |

**Name:** _____   **Date:** _____

# PLANET SCRAMBLE

The names of these planets have been scrambled.
Write the planet names in the blank spaces underneath.

sMra

_____

ipuJret

_____

nurtaS

_____

harEt

_____

yurrecM

_____

senuV

_____

petNenu

_____

Name: _____    Date: _____

## MILLION DOLLAR WORDSEARCH

Circle four items that cost a million dollars or more from the
*How to Spend A Billion* book.

| D | E | H | S | N | L | P | N | O |
|---|---|---|---|---|---|---|---|---|
| O | A | K | W | J | D | A | H | R |
| E | L | T | E | R | I | N | C | Y |
| S | H | I | P | A | F | D | V | G |
| C | A | K | I | S | L | A | N | D |
| S | N | E | L | U | E | S | K | B |
| D | O | F | B | Y | R | E | A | N |
| S | P | A | C | E | S | U | I | T |

Write the words you find below.

_____    _____    _____    _____

Name: _____     Date: _____

# TWO OF A KIND

Cut out the pictures and turn them face down. Take turns to match a pair.
The person with the most pairs wins.

Name: _____     Date: _____

# WRITE YOUR OWN SCRIPT

Use these speech bubbles to write out part of a new graphic fiction story using your own script. What would you make the characters say?